THE SCREAM WRITER'S HANDBOOK

HOW TO WRITE A TERRIFYING SCREENPLAY IN 10 BLOODY STEPS

By
Thomas Fenton

© 2018

Contents

Step 1: What's the big idea!?	1
Step 2: Get Yourself Organized	6
Step 3: Develop Your Process	14
Step 4: Create Meaningful Characters	20
Step 5: Mind the Rule of Three	31
Step 6: Scenes that Scare	35
Step 7: The First Draft	41
Step 8: Schedule to Complete	63
Step 9: Gather Notes and Feedback	67
Step 10: Get your Draft ready for the world…	73
Titles	77
Tips and Tricks	82
Other Valuable Reads	85
Just for Fun	87
55 things I learned not to do from horror movies	88
Parting Words	96
SAW IV Script Excerpt	98

Just a quick word before we begin...

Man, I wish I had this book when I started writing. When I started and was dying to learn the craft, all the books I could find had a few things in common.

One, they were way too long.

Two, they made me sleepy.

Three, whoever wrote them never sold a script in his/her life.

And finally, four, they didn't speak to what I wanted to be. A working screenwriter. And that's why I wrote this book.

If I've done my job by writing this book, I will leave you with the insight and path to writing a terrifying horror script that took me 18 years of working in

Hollywood to figure out. These are hard-won lessons, and I don't mind passing them on.

I value my scar tissue; I find it beneficial. I think you might too.

And here's where I drop my guard and beg you, dear reader, for a favor, if you've bought this book and followed the steps and those steps have led to massive success in the world of film. I have one request.

Hire me.

Horror, what is it?

The first time I was ever scared at the movies (so I was told) was when Ebenezer Scrooge fell through the bottomless grave that led into hell; the film was Scrooge. That was 1970, and I was a little kid then. I know that shows my age, but I don't care, George Lucas made Star Wars for my friends and me, so I'm cool with it.

My mother told me that, when Scrooge was sent screaming down that vortex, I tried to crawl under the seat. I do remember that scene, but not much more. Being scared when you're a little kid sticks with you. I think my mom and dad learned a lesson from that movie and didn't take me to any more scary movies after that, well, until *Jaws*. I lived on Lake Ontario, in a quiet suburb of Rochester, NY. The home of Kodak and the birthplace of motion picture film. Our house's backyard was the Great Lake, and let me tell you, bud… after seeing *Jaws*, I went nowhere near the lake that summer… or the summer after.

These two examples put me on the trail of *Halloween*,

Susperia, Last House On The Left, Nightmare on Elm Street, Poltergeist, The Exorcist, Night of the Living Dead, Friday the 13th, When A Stranger Calls, The Entity, Alien, Legend of Hellhouse, I Spit On Your Grave, The Amityville Horror, The Thing, The Shining, The Fog, Fright Night, Sleepaway Camp, The Howling and *Near Dark* just name a few good Friday night viewings.

Now, watching all these great movies led me to believe that I could join the fray and spill some blood of my own. I made super 8 movies with my friends in the backyard at the shores of the lake. They didn't have the biggest nor best production value, but they had a heart. As I got older and wanted to write, I knew it was going to be a steep mountain to climb, not only because I was from Rochester, NY and knew not a soul in the industry, but I am dyslexic. And with a learning disability of that sort, literally, the last thing you should be is a writer. And as evidence of my affliction, this book you're reading went through the proofing process multiple times, and I bet a few typos still slipped through. It's not the proofreaders' fault nor the publisher's, but my own funky way of spelling and my strange use of grammar. This learning disability should have stopped me in my proverbial tracks, but thanks to a loving, caring family; I turned that negative challenge into something positive. And I wouldn't get rid of this learning disability that makes me spell bed with a 5, for all the tee in Chinese.

So back to blood spilling; in Hollywood, that's a prerequisite, spilling your blood and plenty of it if you ever want to see your name on the big screen. To chase this dream, I went to film school but learned nothing, an expensive "nothing" at that. I then worked as a grip/key grip on a variety of films, including *Lady in White, Night Trap* and *Slaughter of the Innocence*. I learned the trade of film from the c-stand up.

The fact that I had started my career in a below the line position was a novelty in Hollywood. Whilst on the set of *Chain Letter*, I was told by one of the grips that he had heard that I was also part of the brotherhood of Matthews and that I was his inspiration to write. They called him, Buddha. He was cool. I don't know if he ever finished his script, hope he did. Buddha, if you're reading this, drop a brother a line.

So not being the college type, I bought books, *mucho* books. I would try to read them, really, I would. But I didn't want to read; I wanted to write! I know studying is an important part of any learning process, but must the books be sooooo boring? I mean, come on! Aren't we here to create, not read? Let's just get on with it! So, that's what did, I got on with it. I made a ton of mistakes, and many of them are chronicled here, some aren't, but it's like I told my last wife, "I never drive faster than I can see." Besides, it's all in the reflexes.

For ten years I wrote my butt off, managed to sell a comic book series called, *The Dominion*. Did lots of *takes* for production companies; more on takes later. I was then fortunate enough to turn a few specs into sales that would allow me to add my voice to the most popular horror franchise of all time, *Saw*.

I then went on to work on the *I Spit on Your Grave*

franchise. I continue to work in the medium, and as of the publishing of this book, I am in the beginning stages of doing a loose remake of one of the films that I mentioned a few paragraphs ago. I'd have loved to say the title, but at the moment, I can't. I'm sure by the time this book comes out, things will have changed, but today they haven't.

I hope you bought this book to learn from a writer who was and is working in the business of horror. I commend your decision to read this book and to take the knowledge that's held within it to better your career. I've already spilled enough blood for both of us, so let's hope you don't have to spill as much.

The book includes my insights, thoughts and some odd stories that were painful when they were happening but are funny now. I guess time does heal wounds. Also, most of the executives in those stories live now in states like Arizona and Ohio, selling lawn furniture and car insurance nowadays. God Bless them.

A copy of this book, *The Scream Writer's Handbook* is akin to sitting down and having coffee with someone who may know a thing or two. So let's chat if you want… I take my coffee black, and a scone may be nice.

Thanks.
Thomas Fenton
Hollywood Hills, 2018

Step 1:

What's the big idea!?

★ ★ ★

Don't find the right idea, let the right idea FIND you. And, of course, it will if you let it. I'm sure you have tons of ideas. In that mess in your head of creative thoughts, there are good ideas and better ideas, what's most important is to collect those ideas.

We call that a "story dump" or a "story drop." In a classic sense, that means a folder filled with cocktail napkins, scraps of paper and post-its with everything you've ever thought of, or that's come to you.

Got a cool name... Indle Kane? Write it down.

Got an idea for a cool location... a space station orbiting Venus maybe?

Write it down.

Write it all down.

There are no bad ideas in writing, just weak ones.

And what makes a weak idea and what makes a strong one...? Who f*cking knows? The proof is always in the pudding, and since you're the cook, that's up to you.

Now, the idea of evil incarnate killing innocent babysitters on Halloween Night seems like a simple, yet a mythic idea. Or how about four film students disappearing in the woods, and then their footage being found a year later? It sounds pretty cool, or it could be a real sh*t show.

If you're talking about making your own movie, well that's one thing, like *The Blair Witch Project*. This book is about writing a scary horror movie (a movie, not a film, there's a distinction here) so because of that; we're going to stay focused on the task at hand, writing.

The idea has to be big and what I call 'tasty.' It has to be something that can fill the 119 pages or less. But not too much to where you're throwing in the kitchen sink to make it work.

Cool ideas:

"A child's doll is possessed by the soul of a dead serial killer."

"A young girl opens a puzzle box that's a key to the door to hell."

"A great white shark parks off a beach and feeds on hapless tourists."

All small ideas that have both a wide canvas and a deep ocean (*Jaws* pun intended). And by the way, *Jaws* is technically a creature feature, but it's my favorite movie, so it gets a mention, or two.

Familiar with a Twist?

One approach to a fresh idea is putting a twist on the horror tropes that are so plentiful. EX: You can take *Child's Play* and add a twist. Make the doll the hero of the movie. Or take the classic idea of the cabin in the woods and place it in a science fiction setting and you're suddenly Joss Whedon – well not just that, but you get the idea.

Remember, it's cool to stand on the back and shoulders of giants, to add your stone to the top of a pyramid.

Whatever that idea is that you feel like you want to pursue, make one thing non-negotiable... it's a film you'd pay 100 bucks to see. Honest. Write the film YOU'D like to see. The one that will <u>scare the sh*t out of you</u>, an idea so cool that you would have to see it no matter what.

Trying to guess what the market wants is a fool's errand; it will only lead you down the primrose path (bonus points if you can tell me what that's from). Anyway, if you've read this far, I assume a few things.... One, you like horror films and two, you want to write one that's really, really scary.

The best ideas are noisy. That's what they call it. Noisy, I call it tasty, they call it noisy. You know what a noisy idea sounds like? I'll tell you. Years ago, I set up a script at

Beacon Films called *Prodigal Son*. It was to be produced by Twisted Pictures, the same guys that would produce *Saw* a year later. Anyway, I kinda sold this film on its "noisy" concept. And here it is, "*Prodigal Son* is the story about a freelance exorcist who comes to realize that he's the Anti-Christ." See that's a cool idea, if I do say so myself, because it trades in on genre specifics, exorcists and demons, and the Anti-Christ is the hero of the piece. That's taking the known and turning it on its head.

I mean the devil, as the hero? That's noisy.

The next thing I want to talk about is this simple truth. Write what scares you. And when I say "you" I mean, specifically you. This is key. You'll write a great film if it's personal. Each of us is different. Each of us has a different life and different fears.

If you're a mom or a dad, having someone take your child from you, like in *Prisoners*, is the height of terror. If you're a teenager, and like camping, *Grizzly* will scare the bejesus out of you… wait, what? You don't know *Grizzly*? It's *Jaws* in the forest, you know, with a bear. It's awesome, check it out.

Back to my point, personal is the only way to go. They always say write what you know, but fortunately, not a lot of us know killer dolls and dream stalkers. So, we have to reach down into that pit of darkness, some call it our imagination others our personal h*ll, and conjure something to the surface.

Once you have the idea, it's time to get to work.

Exercises

Step 1: What's the big idea?

★ ★ ★

1. Build your story drop file. Collect, in one spot (digital or physical), all your ideas. Collect notes, post-its, napkins, and put in one place as a point of reference.

2. Write down 5 characters for your movie. Write a few bullet points or a paragraph about each, including their names, age, key traits, etc.

3. Write down the top 3 things that scare the sh*t out of you. Be specific. (EX: When the clock rings 12 o'clock on the evening of a full moon). After writing what it is, then write WHY it scares you (scary memory, a memory from a movie). Be specific.

4. Write down three scary scenes you've seen or thought of from a movie that terrified you. In 2-3 lines, what happens in the scene? And in 2-3 more sentences, how does/did that scene scare you?

Step 2:

Get Yourself Organized

★ ★ ★

So, you have your story drop (or dump) loaded with ideas and thoughts. Cool! That's the first thing you need to get organized. Now, you have to turn that gaggle of ideas into something that can generate pages.

Being organized is really important at this stage of the game because it will provide you with the momentum to get through the dreaded first draft. The best way to build that momentum is to use a few crucial steps – these steps differ a bit from the traditional approach that I've seen mentioned in other books where they have you *card, beat sheet, outline, then synopsis, treatment* then when you're all tuckered out and don't care anymore, *the draft.*

Remember, this is a book written by a guy that writes for a living. There's no difference between you and me; I'm just more practiced and streamlined. And this is the way I do things; I like to get to work, so the process that works best for me gets right to business: I like to *card*, *beat sheet* then the *draft*.

It all begins with carding.

Index cards are huge with me. Even with programs like Final Draft and Scrivener, a hard copy of index cards hung on the wall, or placed on the table, is essential. It keeps you attached to your story in a tactile way.

So what goes on the cards? Anything and everything. It doesn't have to be scenes, it can be, but it doesn't have to be. It can be simple "story beats" – just thoughts you have in mind to propel the story.

If you take every idea you have and card it, and by the end of the afternoon, you have 10 cards. And using the *Rule of Three* (we talk about that later), you probably have 30 pages of your script figured out. The cards let you switch scene positions and plot your story's pacing.

An additional trick I use is to write scary scenes and big scenes in *red pen*; this helps me to see if the script is dragging in places visually. If I have a red card every second to third card, I know from the get-go, it won't be a slow script.

From this work of carding, we gather a *beat sheet*, and we do this because we're tidy and kind of lazy. We don't want to just keep laying out the cards on our tables. Once we have the beat sheet written, we can start filling it in with all kinds of stuff, like dialogue and action lines. Remember, your beats may actually be sequences and not full-blown scenes, as a single beat represents an important moment in your story but doesn't necessarily need to be limited to one scene.

> **INT. HAUNTED HOUSE**
>
> Find cellar
> Leads to bones
>
> Make Charlie funny/scared of dark
> (set up as hero - what kind of hero is scared of the dark?)
>
> Things on ceiling grow up into floor - black "mold like"

If you search the Internet for beat sheets – you see a lot of examples with things like "Opening Image" "Set up" and "Catalyst," "Debate" and "Theme Stated," that's not the way I do beat sheets. The academic way of a beat sheet just doesn't jive with me; I'm not casting aspersions, it's just not my thing. It seems to me those kinds of beat sheets are only cool *after* you've seen the movie. I'm writing this movie, man, not watching it. I list the scenes and stuff I want in the script.

Here's an example, if I was writing Poltergeist, it might look something like this:

* * *

Poltergeist

Beat Sheet

Opening with TV signing off – (TV's a running theme in the movie)

We meet the young family at night through the family dog, E-Buzz.

Carol Anne talks with TV People. Family sees this. WTH!

Next Morning – suburban American Dad and pals watch the game.

Normal life.

Fight with a neighbor over control of the remote. Fun!

Diane finds the bird, dead. Foreshadowing?

Robbie and tree. Climbing.

Establish tree as *presence*.

Robbie sees the storm coming.

Bury bird in a cigar box – more family we like!

That night – storm. Closet light. Robby is afraid of lightning.

Clown beat!

See Diane with Steve; they love each other. Smoke some grass.

Kids are afraid of lightning.

Kids sleep with Mom and Dad at night.

Carol Anne more TV – hand comes out at her.

TV people enter the house.

Carol Anne – "They're here."

★ ★ ★

That's the first act of the movie – in beat sheet form.

It doesn't look like there's a lot to it, and there really

isn't. It's ideas for each scene and the *point* of each of those scenes. It's a loose guide to where you want to go. I'd like to point out something that's very important in the above beat sheet. Layered in the first act is the time we're given to grow to like these characters. So, when Diane is swimming in the pool with corpses, we're flipping out for her. It seems like, after the past six years, the "get to know you" scenes in horror films take place in the first 5 minutes, usually whilst driving in a car to the new house, the old cabin on the lake or the cemetery.

And I know why the writers want to get to the scares ASAP – but without caring about the characters, the scares will fall flat. So meaningful character introductions take some time, maybe not the full first act, but give them a chance to bloom.

I try not to make my beat sheets too dense and over thought that I lose interest. I do like to keep some sense of discovery while writing the draft; that keeps things fresh. And when you're writing horror, you rely on those dark times and darker thoughts to deliver the scares, and sometimes that stuff can't be planned, it just happens.

A dear friend of mine, Penn Densham (*Robin Hood: Prince of Thieves*), told me it's best "not to ever face a blank page." And he was right because that's where the beat sheet comes in handy. The beat sheet will provide you with "Islands of Sanity," (another Densham invention) translation: a place you know you're going and all you have to do is swim there.

And if you want, you can take the beat sheet and

expand it with more dialogue and deeper action, and ultimately what you'll have if you want, is an *outline*. I've seen some outlines as long as 40 pages long. Like I said before, I like to keep things loose, so no long outlines for me. I like a sense of fun and danger; it keeps me frosty.

The last thing I want to talk about is "pages." I kept this until last because this is something you may do for an assignment. When I got hired to write a film, I got in and gave them a "take" that's short for a "story take." This happened to me on *Saw*, and *I Spit on Your Grave 2*, the producers wanted to know how I would advance their story, they asked me for a "take."

By the way, they go out to *mucho* writers for takes, so when coming in with your take, you're one of a dozen-plus writers trying to get the same gig. The competition for gigs is fierce, trust me. So when you lock down the gig, the next task is the pages.

Pages are really a "treatment," but since it's for someone else's story, you have to do it, and it's a pain in the butt. Me, I'd rather go to the draft. This is just my failing at treatment writing; it's not my strong suit. Why? Because it deflates and removes my sense of discovery – that darkness that makes scripts great is plotted in pages, so when draft time rolls around, it's all kind of figured out.

When I was on a film called *Zombies Vs. Robots*, the producer asked me to do pages so he and the rest of the team could track my thoughts and ideas, and I fought back, but he made a good point. When working with others, like producers, the pages are the only way they can see right into your mind/project. So if they hire you, you have to do that kinda stuff for the good of the project.

For much of my career, I preferred to work at night. When I lived in Laurel Canyon, it was a woody setting, and one felt really alone. At night, when the house was quiet, and I'd have the mood music playing I would find such a dark place I would literally scare myself sh*tless. So much so that I bought a "rear view mirror" and mounted it on my computer so I could see if anything was behind me. It was my cousin who pointed out that maybe what was stalking me from behind wouldn't show up in the mirror. That didn't help.

It's important to remember, the last thing you do is write. The bulk of your time, the time you spend driving to work, waiting for coffee, during staff meetings you're thinking about what you're going to write. Typing into a computer or typewriter if you're old school, is the last thing you do.

The act of creation takes time.

I wish I was Aaron Sorkin (an extremely talented non-horror writer) who just sits down and blasts his materials out. That would be so cool if I could do that, or Stephen King. That would be awesome. Unfortunately, my process puts me through the ringer before it puts me on the screen. For me, it's work and a lot of it.

But it's damn fun stuff.

Exercise

Step 2: Get Yourself Organized

★ ★ ★

Select three scary ideas or scenes from your story drop file and build a card for each of them. Reference the card example in this chapter to build your card. Each could use any or all of the following: location details (physical surroundings, time of day), characters involved, action, and critical dialogue. These three cards could become part of your first draft down the road, so spending time crafting each card thoughtfully is worth it.

Step 3:

Develop Your Process

★ ★ ★

This chapter is about what is called "your process" not to be confused with "your muse." Your process is a collection of steps and setup which you go through to get to the muse. For some reason, my muse is male, his name is Irv, and when he tells me things, he sounds like he smokes. He coughs *waaaay* too much. Your muse probably sounds better and is friendlier. Lucky you!

So back to the issue at hand, your process. In short, your process is your workflow. After all, screenwriting is a job. I know, I know writing isn't lifting bales of hay or pulling King Crab out of the Bering Strait, but it's work. A good friend of mine once said, "There's nothing more exhausting than constant thought."

Everyone's process is different; no two writers work alike. Some like to write in the early morning before the kids are up and the sun is shining. Some like to write late into the night when the world's quiet and asleep. Like I said before, I used to work that way, starting work around 10 pm – but then I got too busy to be that choosy about my work times, and trained myself or "adjusted my process" to accommodate a larger, more intense workload.

Let's talk about the basics of building a process. Your new "writing job" deserves every chance it can have to succeed. I'm sure this is talked about in other books, but I would be remiss if I didn't at least touch this subject.

At this very minute, I'm sitting at a Coffee Bean & Tea Leaf in Los Feliz, California. I left my beautiful home in the Hollywood Hills, just below the "D" to come here and work. Why? Because it's part of my process. Working in a coffee shop is less distracting than working at home, even with people milling about and music playing, it is. Here, my cat (Geddy) isn't begging me for food or a belly rub, and I can't play my online tank battle game because I'd get killed on this little MacBook Air.

Also, and this is important:

I'm not too comfortable.

I'm sitting in a hard, plastic chair typing on my MacBook. Being out of my element, and being a tad...tad, mind you, uncomfortable, makes me write better. That's part of my process.

Weird I know... but it works for me.

It works well. If you've ever seen an epic documentary called *American Movie*, Mark Borchart, the hero of the film, is attempting to make a horror film. And his process is going to the local airport and sitting in his car to work. Because, as he says, "You can't just stop working and make a pizza, you're stuck in this car, you have to work." I truly feel that everyone needs their car. And oddly enough, according to an article in *The Atlantic* dated Jun 20, 2012, entitled "Study of the Day: Why Crowded Coffee Shops Fire Up Your Creativity," a little noise and commotion are good for the creative soul.

Develop a process that works for you.

If you're not into going into public spaces to write, then work from home. In that case, find a desk away from clutter and noise (the opposite of a coffee shop), and eliminate everyday distractions and set up shop. A card table in the spare bedroom works great, make that your writing place. A place you can go and work for a few hours without being interrupted. The point is to settle into your "workplace" and begin to create.

Writing is like any muscle in your body. The more you use it, the better and stronger it gets, and better results appear. There hasn't been a day in the past 18 years that I didn't write. Now, I'm not talking Stephen King-style writing, where he writes every day except for Christmas and his wife's birthday, I'm talking about notes, thoughts, research, and writing. Remember, sitting down to write your script is literally the last thing you do.

For me, music is also an important part of my process.

This is so common; it's not really worth mentioning, but I will. Playing the *Hellraiser* soundtrack while you create your horror masterpiece can only help things. So, if you do go to the coffee shop or work in a bustling spot, bring a pair of headphones. As I said at the beginning of this chapter, everyone's process is different; you need to find what works for you.

Remember, the easiest words for any writer are: FADE IN. The hardest words are FADE OUT.

Exercises

Step 3: Develop Your Process

★ ★ ★

To successfully establish a process that works for you, test out a few variations to see where you find yourself most creative and productive. Over the next several days, test out and hone in on the best location, time of day and define your necessary tools to be most successful.

1) Location – at home, or away from home. <u>Home:</u> Find a spare room or space you can designate for your writing sessions, away from distractions of others and everyday life. Set up a table and chair and get to work. <u>Away from home:</u> Find a coffee shop, park or spot where you can set up at a table and spend at least one uninterrupted hour (or two) working.

2) Time of Day – some of us are most creative first thing in the morning, so get up an hour early and test your energy then. Others do

better in the evening. After you find a location that works, find the sweet spot for your creative energy by testing out your process; morning, noon and night. Spend an hour in each day part on different days to see which works best. I recommend writing no more than 3-4 hours on any given day. Personally, I do my best work 1-2 hours at a go, for each project I'm working on.

3) Tools – always travel with the following: Story Drop folder, Final Draft 10 and/or Scrivener, laptop lock, headphones, pen and paper for notes.

Step 4:

Create Meaningful Characters

★ ★ ★

"Character is what you are in the dark."
– Dwight Lyman Moody

This is where the rubber hits the road. It's all about character. You can have the best setup in the world, and the coolest plot, but if you don't have characters that people like, like I said before, the whole thing will fall as flat as a bloody pancake.

Do you think anyone would have given a toss about Laurie Strode if she wasn't such a lovable babysitter who wouldn't let Tommy stay up too late? What about the Freelings? Without liking them, why should we care if they got Carol Anne out of the damn TV?

Years ago when I was working with a big-time producer, I visited him at his office at Columbia Pictures (I call it Columbia, not Sony, I'm old school like that) where he told me, to my face, that my scripts were great and really fun to read, but were lacking in the character department. I was shocked of course, shocked! How could that be? My work had the story points I needed, the pacing was good, and the plot was solid. "Yeah," he said while meeting me in the eye, "but who gives a sh*t if we don't care about the characters?"

Now, instead of getting all defensive and "you don't know what you're talking about," I sat back and listened to what the producer had to say. I figured "If this cat is going to take the time to read my stuff and give it some thought, I better be open to hear what he has to say." So, as we strolled the stages of the storied studio, he gave me notes which I have used to this day. The same notes I am relaying to you now, dear reader.

When writing a story, and this is a starting point: base the characters on someone you *know* or *have known*. I say this knowing full well that if you wrote *Halloween* and knew a Michael Myers in the past, I reckon you're lucky to be breathing. I'm not talking about the killers or the ghosts; we're not asking the audience to care about them. They're the ones we fear, not the ones we care about.

The "to be tortured" – the center of your scares, you know, the ones that rented the cabin for the weekend, or the ones that inherited the creepy old house on the hill, those should (at first) be the ones based on your personal reality. As the drafts move on, I'm sure you'll splinter way from this rule, but believe me, it's a good place to start.

This is also connected to your use of the character's dialogue. Dialogue is the tool our characters use to tell us about themselves and others. It's the audiences' main source of information in the movie.

Dialogue is something you should start studying, right now, the moment you finish reading this book. No one talks the same, and everyone's cadence is different. Use your ear to capture that. It takes time, but it's doable.

Ever notice a character who calls another character by name whilst in a scene together?

> Nikki
> Kerry, what do you mean?

> Kerri
> You know what I mean, Nikki.

> Nikki
> No, I don't Kerry.

> Kerri
> Yes, you dooo Nikki!

Do you do that in real life? Talk to your friend by calling them by name to their face, over and over again… while they're standing in front of you? No, you don't… unless you're a psychopath, which I really hope you aren't.

This "name calling craziness" happens for a reason: the screenwriter wants to keep track of who's who within the scene. And a lazy writer thinks the best way of doing that is to have each character call one another by name, creating a painful exchange. So, don't do that, please.

Now, on to character arcs – so let's say you've based a character on an old girlfriend or boyfriend and you know their cadence and the words they'd speak. Those are the good, healthy bones to start building a character. So now what? It's important that each character have an established arc throughout the story. Each character should have a purpose, a starting point (emotionally, physically, psychologically), a journey with scenes that influence their psyche, and by the end of the story, they land in a new place because of how the story changes them.

Take Martin Brody from *Jaws* as an example. Martin's a tough cop from New York who's moved his family to Amity Island for a better life, but the thing is, he's afraid of the water. The shark puts Martin through his journey that ends with him slugging it out with a massive great white shark while stranded on the high seas.

The characters of a horror movie run the gamut – but they all have one thing in common:

The hero must taste blood.

It's MacReady saving the ice station in *The Thing*. It's Nancy setting up traps and confronting Freddy in *Night on Elm Street*. The hero had to take his journey, I mean, if he didn't, we wouldn't have a movie, at least not one I'd pay to watch.

Here, I'd like to recommend a book; it's *The Hero's Journey: Joseph Campbell*.

Understanding what Campbell's talking about will

make your writing less of a bug hunt and more of a stand-up fight.

The basic steps in the hero's journey are (excerpted from &/or my interpretation of *The Hero's Journey: Joseph Campbell*):

THE ORDINARY WORLD

Heroes live in their world. At home watching TV, or working at the video store. We see them in their ordinary world, and it's kind of boring. That said, the hero is an outsider, someone that possesses something unique that can cause them pain but can also make them great!

In Halloween, Laurie Strode as she babysits Tommy.

In Saw, Dr. Gordon as he tends to his patients.

Katie in IS2 as she tries to get her modeling career going.

THE CALL TO ADVENTURE

For the heroes to get on with their journeys, there needs to be a call to adventure. This might be an event or a piece of knowledge that thrusts them into the story. Basically, they get thrown into the deep end, away from their typical world. But they do, at the end of the day, accept their quest.

Campbell tells us that heroes get a mystic object to help them on their journey, like the microcassette in *Saw*. In some cases, heroes happen upon their quest by accident. Campbell puts it like this, "A blunder — the merest chance — reveals an unsuspected world."

Campbell describes this new world as a "fateful region of both treasure and danger...a distant land, a forest, a kingdom underground, beneath the waves, or above the sky, a secret island, lofty mountaintop, or profound dream state...a place of strangely fluid and polymorphous beings, unimaginable torments, superhuman deeds, and impossible delight" Pg. 48.

The Clark called to investigate *Event Horizon*.

Ash and company spend the weekend in the cabin in the woods in *The Evil Dead*.

REFUSAL OF THE QUEST

One thing that makes the film more fun to watch is when the heroes refuse the call of adventure. It's a no-brainer that they go forth and kick – ass, but being the real humans that they are, they hesitate. When this happens, the stage is set for a total disaster. There's a reason for which the powers-that-be have chosen a particular hero. A refusal of the quest can only be big trouble... (in little china).

Alex Kintner killed in *Jaws*.

Dallas being killed in the tunnels of the Nostromo in *Alien*.

ACCEPTING THE CALL

Once the adventure is accepted, the heroes advance into the next stage of their journey.

ENTERING THE UNKNOWN

As they embark on their journey, the heroes enter a world they have never experienced before. Very often, it is filled with supernatural creatures, breathtaking sights, and the constant threat of death. This place is unlike the heroes' home, this outside world has its own rules, and they best learn to respect these rules, or they get their butts kicked. After all, it is not the end of the journey that we're watching (and writing about), but the journey itself.

Father Karras helping Father Merrin with the exorcism in *The Exorcist*.

Kirsty going after her father in *Hellraiser II*.

SUPERNATURAL AID

Supernatural doesn't have to mean magical. As a genre writer, you live in a world of the supernatural, or "above the laws of nature." Heroes are put on the journey by someone who's mastered the laws of the outside world and can give them the wisdom to go forth. Sometimes, the character often gives them something that will help them complete their quest; sometimes it's just wisdom, and at other times, it's an object.

As Campbell says, "One has only to know and trust, and the ageless guardians will appear." The job of the supernatural assistor is to give the heroes what they need to finish the quest—not finish it for them.

Hellraiser: The Puzzle Box

Babadook: The Book

ALLIES/HELPERS

Every hero needs a helper, much like every superhero needs a sidekick. Without the assistance of their companions and helpers and allies along the way, most heroes would fail miserably. It's like Lennon said, "I get by with a little help from your friends."

Tangina in *Poltergeist*.

Jack in *An American Werewolf in London*.

TESTS and THE SUPREME ORDEAL

The heroes go through all kinds of mess to get stronger and sharper in order to get ready for the final showdown. These tests are essential for the hero's journey.

When it comes down to it, all the toil and trouble comes into play. Once this obstacle's overcome, the tension will be relieved. The worst has passed, and the quest, while not officially over, has succeeded.

Rosemary's Baby – Rosemary gives birth.

The Shining – Danny loses Jack in the Maze.

REWARD AND THE JOURNEY HOME

Most of the time, there's a reward given to heroes for passing the "Supreme Ordeal." Maybe it's a Kingdom;

maybe it's a medal… or maybe it's a coupon for a Royale with Cheese.

Whatever it is, it's a reward for the journey.

And sometimes, even the journey home can be a test. Just because the Supreme Ordeal is over, it doesn't mean it's smooth sailing.

Saw: Gordon cuts off his foot to escape bathroom.

Alien: Ripley escapes the Nostromo.

MASTER OF TWO WORLDS/ RESTORING THE WORLD

In the end, the heroes' quest is life-changing. They've saved their world (the ordinary one). Many times, they return with "the elixir," an object or personal ability that allows them to save their world.

The heroes have also grown to be badasses. They've not only overcome the Supreme Ordeal, but they've conquered their own fears. Now, they're worthy of being king, or sheriff maybe even dungeon master.

Saw: Amanda becomes Jigsaw's apprentice

The Evil Dead: Ash is now king

★ ★ ★

This is indeed classic storytelling stuff; it's ageless and

mythic. But you might ask yourself, what does this have to do with writing a terrifying screenplay? Well, I'll tell you... you, my friend, are writing the new mythos. Isn't that who and what Michael Myers is... the devil? The boogeyman? What about Freddie...the new Morpheus? These are legends in the making, and to some (like me) they have already achieved that status.

One of the major distinctions of writing horror, specifically in the process of creating characters, is that you have to write to consider your *body count* in your character count and descriptions. You know who I'm talking about, *body count,* they are the unfortunate characters in a horror film; they don't have an arc and hardly do a damn thing, they just get wiped out in one evil way or another.

Although I'm not a huge fan of this concept, a terrifying horror film generally needs victims, but I do think every (single) body should have some meaning or mention. You can do this by making each character interesting by peppering in little motifs, weaknesses, and strengths.

After investing your heart and soul in building your robust cast of characters, they become almost like children to you. They're your creation, and now, you must wipe them out. Don't be afraid to kill what you created. As the writer you're God, at least their God, so don't be afraid to deliver a little wrath. And make sure you kill them off in cool, unexpected ways.

The audience will thank you for it.

Exercises

Step 4: Create Meaningful Characters

★ ★ ★

1. Spend 10 minutes when you are next waiting in line, put your phone down and listen intently. Take a moment to hear how the person near you delivers their message, conveys information. What words did they use? How did they structure their thought or message? What emotion did they use? Pick one sentence you hear and write it down. Now rewrite it the way you would have said it. Now write the way your best friend might say the same message. Interesting, right?

2. Pick three characters that you drafted in Step 1 Exercises, and start to flesh them out in two or three paragraphs. Think about what they might look like, age, their dress, background, what they do for a living, mannerisms and lastly their cadence. Think about what role they'll in your screenplay.

Step 5:

Mind the Rule of Three

★ ★ ★

It's way, way too common to overwrite your first draft. That is to say, way too many words and way too many pages to say *way* too little. You may think it takes nine pages to get through the scene where the character decides to stay and fight the ghost. If you start to use the "Rule of Three" I guarantee you'll trim your page count and make your dialogue more potent.

What's the "Rule of Three?" Well, first it's more of a guide than a rule, but here it is:

★ ★ ★

RULE OF THREE

Every three pages, something needs to happen.
No scenes should be longer than three pages.
Dialogue should be held to three lines.

Action should also be held to three lines.

and

Write three pages every day.

* * *

What is this, you say? Three, only three? Is that it? No, that's not it. It's a place to start; it's a *rule* to keep in the back of your mind while you create. It's not a law, but a rule. Now, we all agree there will be a lot of rewriting, but the *Rule of Three* will help keep those drafts reined in.

You're less likely to have a run-on script using the *Rule of Three*.

If every page of a script is roughly a minute on screen, and to keep a horror fan (some of the savvier fans on the planet) on edge, something needs to happen, and the scene should change every three pages to keep the story moving and the viewer engaged.

Keep each chunk of dialogue to three lines or less. Overloading on dialogue is one of the most common tendencies for beginning screenwriters. Remember, it's called *dialogue*, not *monologue*, and the exchange between characters is critical and every word intentional, so the Rule of Three will soon become a habit and not too difficult to follow once you get the hang of it.

Can there be scenes and dialogue over three lines? Yes, there are exceptions, look at *Saw*, Billy the Puppet would talk for pages, but as William Shakespeare once said, "Brevity is the soul of whit."

And that goes double, for action lines – they really need to stay within three lines, or like me, if you need some more punch, *two paragraphs of three lines*. In this instance, I recommend the writing of Walter Hill or Shane Black; both are experts at motion and action.

And lastly, write your script three pages at a time. One 3-page scene a day, perhaps two if the mood takes you. In less than 30 days, you'll have a draft. And if you follow the *Rule of Three*, the draft will be in much better shape than if you had just free-wheeled it.

Exercises

Step 5: Mind the Rule of Three

★ ★ ★

1. Print or write, on a post-it note, the *Rule of Three*. Make sure your cat doesn't abscond with it.

2. Put this on your computer or on the top of your story drop folder and keep it visibly nearby every time you write.

3. Down the road, at the beginning of your writing session, when settled into your process, re-read the previous day's work/scene and objectively check your action (3 lines), dialogue (3 lines) and scene length (3 pages or less) to see if it meets the *Rule of Three*.

Step 6:

Scenes that Scare

★ ★ ★

One thing that always amazes me is the idea that you have to write a script in sequence...as in, from start to finish.

The good news is that you don't have to. You can write whatever you want, whenever you want. Sounds obvious, I know but a lot of people think of a story from starting in one place and ending someplace later. When I was working on the *Saw* franchise, I would work backward on an idea. I'd write the crazy twist ending first, then back into the story making sure my starting point was hell and gone from where I needed to end up at the end.

Say for instance, that I want a scene where the ghost chases the hero through the woods. I write that scene. While I write it, I might have a few ideas about how to get into the scene as well. Then, I know that I want it to end with the ghost trapped inside of a crystal ball. I write that scene. Then a few pages later, I want to showcase the origin of the said crystal ball. If I'm using the *Rule of Three*, you now have damn near the first 9 pages of your script.

Basically, write the things <u>you know you need first</u> using the tools in your *Arsenal of Horror* (to be discussed later). And as always, rewrite the scenes to fit better as the draft proceeds, and the story takes firmer shape.

Horror is a wide target.

Unlike comedy which is completely subjective. Example: one guy might find Adam Sandler farting in someone's soup funny, while his date thinks Sandler is stupid and inane. But neither of them chooses to head into the dark basement and face the army of organized and vicious rats that'll attack them. See what I mean? Who would? That's why horror is fun to write; fear is man's first and deepest instinct. Fear is eternal. It's the instinct that kept our species alive when Saber-Tooth Tigers were circling the cave.

Every artist has a tool they have to work with. A painter has his paints, the sculptor has his chisel, and you... the writer have words for tools. And your main tool is *fear*.

SHADES OF FEAR

There are different shades of fear. Fear lives in the gut. It tickles the stomach and makes the hairs on the back of your neck stand up. Fear is the feast that feeds upon your soul.

These are the shades of fear you have to work with:

SUSPENSE

Suspense is the fast beating heart. It's the worry about what's around the corner, and what might be coming from down the road.

ANXIETY

It's waiting for the hammer to fall. Hoping it doesn't, but reacting if it does.

FORESHADOWING

These are signs along the road that things aren't what they seem and that greater darkness lies ahead. The more the signs, the worse things get. And hopefully, the character also sees what we see and worries about their own future. It's the when the old man's warning about the abandoned summer camp is ignored.

DREAD

One of my personal favorites. It's a classic oncoming terror. The dark days are here, and there's nothing that can be done about it. Be careful not to judge dread… get it?

REVULSION

Revulsion is the gross factor. *Saw* uses this a lot…. So does *I Spit*. Come to think of it… jeeez… so did *Chain Letter*. I guess I use this one a lot. Things are bad for the character on screen, and you're thankful it isn't you.

SHOCK

Shock is when the bad guy strikes. Shock doesn't last long and should be used surgically, not when cats jump out at the protagonist whilst searching the old basement. That's more of a *jump scare*. It's when the dream inside the dream becomes real. That's shock.

And that leads us to —

HORROR

Horror is the granddaddy of the emotions, the reason why we're all here. Horror is the culmination of all the other shades of fear. Horror is about the world the characters inhabit. It's about their existence, either for a moment or a lifetime. Maybe the horror is to escape Leatherface or Jigsaw or a lifelong goal to elude the Cenobite's realm of existence.

At its core, horror is anything you think it is. And that's why it's important to write what *you* fear.

If you have a thing about deep dark water, write it.

Don't like old houses, write it.

Don't like spiders, write it.

Writing is your make-believe wants on paper, but it's also *you* on the paper. This is writing 101 – but I have to mention it. It's a big thing, people think you don't have to put yourself on paper when writing horror, but the best ones do. Did you know that Stephen King's book *Misery* is about alcoholism? How about the last *House on the Left* as a metaphor about Vietnam? And that the *Hills Have Eyes* is about <u>not</u> buying a Winnebago?

And as a writer, I can say this, one of the best feelings I've ever had was in Mann's Chinese Theater (in '07) watching *Saw IV* play out to a packed house of fans and hearing them scream in fear.

It's like a roller coaster without having to stand in line. Horror is a communal experience; it's one of a few genres people flock to the theaters to watch with their friends. Sure you can watch horror movies alone, but there's nothing like leaning over to your friend while watching *Scanners* and say, "Did you see the way that guy's head exploded!" It's fun; it's cool. It's worth the drive.

Exercise

Step 6: Scenes that Scare

★ ★ ★

Choose (from Step 1 Exercises) one of your biggest fears to write a terrifying scene about. Using the *Rule of Three*, draft a 3-page scene that includes your primary character, dialogue, action and focuses on one of the shades of fear. Make sure you choose an idea that terrifies you. This will become one of the big scares in your first draft.

Step 7:
The First Draft

★ ★ ★

Okay, boys and girls, this chapter is by far the most important thing I have to tell you. If you bought this book and wanted a few pieces of gold gleaned from its pages, this is it:

WRITE A COMPLETE FIRST DRAFT
NO MATTER F*&KING WHAT!

There, I said it, and I feel good about it. I cannot tell you how many people stumble and fall at this juncture. They get their workspace together, they buy a new computer, they sharpen their pencils, they get their headphones, they download the *Dark Knight* soundtrack, they get to work, and on page two, they can't decide if the killer drives a red car or a blue car. And there, the script dies a quiet, lonely death. So, what went wrong here? Why was the momentum killed?

Because the writer thought it mattered if the car was

blue or if the car was red.

I have news for you, in a first draft NOTHING MATTERS. It's all up for grabs! It's all going to change anyway, in one of the many, many rewrites that lay before you, which we'll talk about later.

"So, Tom," I can hear you thinking, "if the first draft doesn't matter, and it's all going to change anyway, why even do the first draft?" Because, wise-ass, all stories have a beginning. They have to start somewhere, and the first draft (warts and all) is the only place they can begin.

There are a few reasons why some writers never complete the first draft. The most common one is that they want it to be perfect and not have to do any rewriting. That's a b*llshit reason, and it won't hold up in court.

Writing is in the rewriting.

No one does one draft, no one. I used to think I was so good, like *Moe Zart*, I would do one draft, and that was it. You know what? Those drafts sucked. Awful! Every once in a while, I'll get an email from an old friend who threatens to put up his copy of my script 'The Whisper Man" on eBay. I laugh and say, "No one's going to buy it." They continue with the threat, so I end up buying it. Better safe than sorry.

Another reason some writers don't finish the first draft is that they don't want to be judged. I get this one 110%. To this day, I hate turning in a draft and getting notes on it. Painful, but it comes with the territory.

Years ago, on *Prodigal Son*, the movie's producer was Gregg Hoffman (producer of *Saw*), and he had made notes on a draft I'd turned in. One scene he didn't think was so hot; I knew that because he wrote across the page, "Duhhh! This is the worst scene I've ever read." That note nearly killed me the first time I read it, but I have that draft with his notes in my desk to this day. And you know what? I've never written a scene that sh*tty since. Unfortunately, for the world of film, Gregg passed away suddenly in 2005. It was a huge loss to the community and to me, personally. He was a great guy and will be forever missed. His words will always be with me.

In short, fretting about feedback is pointless and no good for your draft. Being afraid of working hard (as in rewriting) is also no good. If you want to write a screenplay, be prepared to work your ass off, and take massive punches in the gut. After all, it comes with the territory.

This is why you have to complete the first draft, even if you *know* it has problems. Once the draft is done, you can (and will) go back and make adjustments. It's far easier to work on a completed draft than a file of pieces and parts. At one time, a guy I coached wanted to write and would only write the first act over and over again until he thought it was perfect. Talk about a momentum killer.

And finally, the last reason a would-be writer doesn't get the first draft done is that if it's *never* finished, it *could* be the best script ever written. And who knows, they might be right.

And since you're writing a horror genre script, it's really important that you keep your script warm and fresh and you do that by working at it. So that's why you want to get the first draft written as soon as possible, but as well as possible. On the next several pages are what I term my "Arsenal of Horror," fundamentals I apply to every script I write.

ARSENAL OF HORROR

Use it well.

RULES OF THE WORLD

"Rules of the World" are super important for you, horror writers, out there. Often, horror writers just sit down and start writing whatever it is that scares them, just like the work I made you do. That's cool, and a good starting point, but eventually you have to incorporate the laws of the world in your writing.

Establishing rules will make your script function as an organic creation because it has guardrails of structure to bounce between and along your writing journey.

I have to be very mindful here not to upset my peers too much, I still work and live in this lovely town. So, I'm not going to point out the crappy and inane examples of films that break the *Rules of the World*. But imagine this, Jigsaw is known as a mechanical genius, and highly intelligent. We kind of root for him because he has to be smart and teach us his lessons. What if we disregard the rules and say that once Jigsaw is trapped by the cops in his lair, he suddenly uses magic, turns into a bird and flies away? How bad would that suck? A scene like that would utterly decimate all the mythos and fear you've created by writing a cheap, lazy beat instead of a *Rules of the World* beat. A beat that respects the world you've established.

Basically, the *Rules of the World* is a way to keep you, the writer, in check. It makes you work harder for your audience. What the rules do for you, is to say to the good movie-watching public, trust me, I know what I'm doing.

Now, someone is thinking, "Tom, what about Michael Myers, huh? What about the ending of *Halloween*? Didn't Carpenter break the *Rules of the World* with that ending?" Don't confuse breaking the rules with a proper twist. At the end of *Halloween* (1978 only), it becomes evident that Michael Myers is something more than human. And that's a twist, not a break of the world's rules. The twist was set up when we learned that Michael was different from others, by Dr. Loomis. Dr. Loomis seems to know exactly what Michael is, and tries to warn others; they just aren't listening. So when, at the end of the picture, Michael is not dead after being shot and falling off the balcony, it makes sense since we had experienced that *foreshadowing*.

COLD OPEN

What is a cold open? And why should I consider using it?

To quote *Dune* "The beginning is a very delicate time." It's the first thing the agents and producers are going to read, and they will, I guarantee you, decide in the first ten pages of the script if they like it, and by the transitive property, also like you.

Well, what a cold open is, is a fantastic way to capture attention from the get-go. Some consider it a *cheat*, that is to say *too much too soon*. I don't always agree. I think if it's written thoughtfully and with intention, you can really do a great deal with the cold open. It's an important part of my arsenal for sure.

For demonstration purposes, in the back of this book are the pages from my original draft of *Saw IV*. I loved the opening and thought it did just what was needed, others didn't entirely agree, but that's show business.

There are a few ways to use the cold open. The first way is to tease the audience about the future state of the character. For instance, if your cold open shows a vortex of evil ripping the heroes to pieces, once the script starts, the viewer will wonder, "What the hell is this vortex thing?" and minds are off to the races trying, for the balance of the movie, to piece together where that opening fits in the story.

Another way to use a cold open is to get some exposition out of the way. You might show the family that was killed in the house before our new family moves in and their journey begins. Thus, setting up via a flashback the foreboding evil that will grow as the story marches on.

The third way is just to kick some ass, chew bubble gum and take some names. As I mentioned before, the cold open is used to tell the reader, "Buckle your seatbelt and hang on; you're in for a crazy ride." This would be making the cold open a seminal scene in the film. Maybe it's the big fight (which you resolve much later in the script), or maybe it's the "*pseudo climax*" of an act. I say pseudo because the scene shown is almost always a false ending. You don't want to give the whole thing away, mostly you want to send the viewer wondering how the story will unfold.

MOTIVATION

Motivation is simply – what the character's after. What do they want from the scene/movie? Make this a valid and obvious point. Sounds like a duh moment, but it's not. Get this sorted out straight away. This is akin to the work on developing each character and their individual arcs. Without an arc, there's no need for the character, and their motivation must be clear to the viewer.

What you don't want is a meaningless, unmotivated character that makes the audience lose trust in what's going on and why. That's never good. If the Werewolf Hunter wants to kill the werewolves that killed her grandmother, make sure we know that from the get-go.

Revenge is always a good motivation. If the young

couple wants their daughter out of the TV, say that too. This work should be all done in the first act.

Usually, the weakness of characters, the thing that they're most afraid of, or their *kryptonite* is the fact that they don't want to die. Simple, right? Sometimes the characters also have their personal kryptonite, their own fears that make their journey harder and more intense.

Like in *Event Horizon*, with each crewmember struggling to survive while being stalked by their own fears. And in the end, they get picked off one by one. Another great example of this can be found in *The Legend of Hell House* and the *Shining*.

Also, what are the consequences of failure? What are the stakes? Is the world at stake? Is mankind? Or is it the family? Make that clear.

ISOLATION

Isolation is a huge tenant of horror films. The hero or heroes must go it alone – physically, spiritually, emotionally and/or psychologically. This is touched on in Campbell's *The Hero's Journey: Joseph Campbell,* but it needs to be amped up here. It's the cabin in the woods. The boat on the ocean. The castle on the hill.

And here's a cool trick. Watch a movie like *The Conjuring* and see how James Wan deals with isolation. A house full of sleeping people becomes very isolating when Mom goes down into the basement.

Sometimes, a simple, closed door or a simple step away from the center of a lively party can be enough to isolate a character to create some terrifying scares. One standout example includes the plethora of suburban horror films that were spawned from *Poltergeist*. The house of horror being part of a normal neighborhood was a new twist on the old tenant about haunted houses and hit too close to home for many a horror fan.

In fact, many, many years ago, I went to the Amityville House and was stunned to see it's in a normal neighborhood. It wasn't isolated off in some swamp somewhere. It had a mailbox and everything!

Also specific to this day and age, isolation means getting rid of cell phones and other personal communication. Isolation is in essence, removing the "lifelines" a hero typically has access to for aid or survival.

TICKING CLOCK

To ramp up suspense and to add in motivation, it's best to have a ticking clock. This is the time set for the hero (es) to complete their task, or the time the great event will take place. Maybe it's staying alive until dawn. Or racing home before sunset. Maybe it's Halloween Night.

The *Pull the Pin* beat, is another way to get your film either started or kick it into high gear. *Saw* would take these beats literally and be massively effective with it.

The ticking clock is so important; I don't think I've ever worked on a script that didn't have one. As the script heads into the 3rd and final act, the clock should be entering its final countdown. This will heavily influence your...

PACING

Pacing is the lifeblood of a script. Tools like the *Rule of Three* and the *Wicked Pass* (which we'll get into in a few pages) are meant to help with that, because pacing is really the call and onus of the writer, and must not be forsaken due to script mechanics or poor editing.

One way to do pace for impact is to change the way you write action scenes. Make them bare bones and right to the point. No extraneous detail. The idea being, the mood, and the style have been established already so that when the zombies attack, man, make sure the reader is as out of breath as your characters are.

SOUND

Imagine being locked in a bathroom, your ankle chained to the radiator. It's pitch black. You can't see sh*t. Which sense must you depend on now? Your hearing. Sound is a large part of your *Arsenal of Horror*; it contributes significantly to experience and fueling fear.

Also, it's a misnomer that creepy sounds happen only in the dark. Think about all the sounds that scare in broad daylight. Something crashes on the floor in the room above you. A door slams shut in a room across the house. The sound of car breaks screaming toward you in your rearview mirror. A car peels out in the street where your child has been playing in the park. A doorbell rings and the doorknob turns, waking you up from a nap on the couch. Every sound and the context it's in can send a chill quickly up someone's spine.

When setting (and carding) a scene, consciously set up the sounds in that scene. Is the glowing yellow light bulb hung on a crooked finger of wire buzzing? What about the wolves off in the hills, howling at the moon, warning us to take cover or die by claws and fang? Is the car door slamming preceded by yelling or infectious laughter?

VILLAINS, CREATURES, AND MONSTERS

There's an old saying, "Your script is only as good as your villain."

As a horror writer, you really have to pay attention to developing a formidable villain. And once again, you're the villain's Creator here, so it can be literally anything! Anything! We know villains that include a doll, a shark, a mute killer, a dead person and even an elevator (check out the 1985 opus *The Lift*).

Your villain needs to be yours and yours alone. I'll admit that by definition, genre villains share certain characteristics. For instance – Jason and Michael are a lot alike, but different in subtle ways that make each individually unique.

Here's a riddle: *Who would win in a fight using only trademark skills, Jason Vorhees or Michael Myers? The answer is, Michael Myers because he can drive and Jason is a momma's boy. Ha!!!!!!*

What about Damian Thorne? He's the bad guy and doesn't look it. Patrick Bateman is the same thing. They're the Devil in disguise. But there should be small, and subtle giveaways, and to me...that giveaway is in the eyes.

The eyes are said to be windows to the soul. And I personally, use them as a mark of distinction. Crystal blue eyes or dull green eyes with small pupils make a statement. Eyes so dark you can't distinguish the pupil from the iris make a different statement. And let's not forget about the glowing eyes or the eyeless sockets...

And for some reason, all my villains (if they speak) have deep voices... I know it seems a bit cliché. But hey, it works for me. Define your villain with a distinctive feature which by association with your character invokes fear. Slightly off skin-tone, odd facial feature or mark, expression or mannerism, voice or cadence unique to your villain with some meaning or backstory attached to it.

HUMOR

Yes, you're reading that right, I said "humor." The topography of a good strong horror script needs to have both hills and valleys. Ups and downs, frights and laughs. Now, I'm not talking about a comedy at all. Just a few moments when the tension lightens up a bit to allow the audience to catch a breath and let their pulse settle down a few beats.

A script that's one long *screeeeeeeam* becomes just that, a lot of noise. It loses its effectiveness. Adding some humor helps the audience come to know and like the characters a bit more as well.

Take Adam from *Saw*; his pretend death scene to placate Jigsaw was funny. What about Evil Ed in *Fright Night*? He's goofy but effective.

The point is, try to relieve some tension by peppering in some lighter material. Don't force the humor, that rarely works, just add some funny and relevant beats or lines of dialogue to create those needed valleys. I'm not a huge fan of making one comic relief typecast character and placing all of your funny-eggs in their basket. It gives that character too much weight and telegraphs to the audience that they are going to "get got." Spread the love to the others, make them all likable, it strengthens the script in many ways.

DON'T BE A WUSS

I think it was Quentin Tarantino who said, "You know a character is cool if you leave the theater acting like him." Spot on.

Audiences don't like wimps, wusses or flakes. They like heroes. Make sure your main character takes action and isn't afraid of getting their hands dirty.

Ash from the *The Evil Dead* is the ultimate "not a wuss" hero. Now, cutting your hand off and replacing it with a chainsaw seems a bit much, but it is pretty cool. Alice from *Friday the 13th*, she cut off Mrs. Voorhees's head!

Make sure you write the hero in a strong voice, don't let them shudder at the sight of blood (unless this is part of the arc). Make sure they don't yell a lot, and talking to themselves is a no-no. Sometimes, characters can do what they call *Sotto Vox*, or "under their breath." I'll write that once in a while, but having the hero or villain talk plot points out loud is another, no-no.

PAGE COUNT

If you don't know anything about this, you should. If you want to go into great depth on this, check out the Syd Field books *The Foundation of Screenwriting*. If I'm 100% honest I think I might have owned the book at some point, and I think I tried to read it, as I mentioned at the beginning of this book, I probably never finished it, and it didn't take. Now, just because I stink at reading those kinds of books, that's my bad, if you need to know structure or more of the academic fundamentals of general screenwriting, you should take a look.

But for those of you that want the super basics, here they are: I use the Three Act structure.

I like my script lengths to ring in about 119 pages at the most. If it's in the 90s, you're not using the pages to their greatest potential. If you're 120+, you're risking being too literal and too descriptive, and frankly it might never be read.

It's all about balance.

A good script has to be light, yet heavy, filled with strong visuals, but not have too many words. It says something, but it's not to be too wordy. Remember, this isn't a novel, so use the words that best create a visual experience for the reader.

ACT I

Many books say ACT I should be 30 pages long. I personally think it should be around 25 pages, in order to keep the pace going, and this works especially well for horror. Act I is the setup for the script; it's the introduction to the world, the characters that inhabit it and establishes your *Rules of the World.*

Set up the motives and missions, introduce all the pertinent characters whom you know and care (one way or another) for. Make sure you're well seeded in the world by the end of the first act.

ACT II

This act is about 60 pages or so. It's the confrontation act, basically where the *f*t hits the shan.* Through all of Act II, the script should continue to rise and the pressure builds.

You'll hear this a lot from other writers that the second act is the biggest pain in the butt. And I tend to agree with them; the first fifteen pages and the last fifteen pages are easy, but the middle part, the icing in the Oreo, is a dangerous place. The reason being, this is where it's really easy to slow the script down to a crawl. I mean, how many times have you heard? "It was a good movie until it dragged a little in the middle." Many times, I'll wager.

So, keep that in mind when writing ACT II. Set up

a lot of interesting roadblocks for your characters to overcome or discover. Make sure to map and plot each character's arc and use this act to ensure you're propelling their growth and evolving them to deliver on their intention and purpose. And don't forget the *Rule of Three* and remember to keep the audience cringing as these lessons and tests unfold in this act.

ACT III

Another 30 pages and the first draft will be complete! Sounds like a lot of work, but if you're paying attention and really worked your ACT II, this act should be a breeze. It's the climax and the conclusion of your script. It's supposed to be like rolling off a log, simple and natural. Unfortunately, many times it isn't, but I hope it is for you.

To make your movie a little more memorable, consider including a Third Act Surprise which is when something unexpected happens that changes the direction of where the ACT III is headed. In *Jaws*, the Third Act Surprise is when Quint, the shark killer, is killed by the shark! It falls onto the Chief (who's afraid of the water) to face his greatest fear whilst on a sinking ship.

WHITE ON THE PAGE

Here's a big secret…and well worth the cost of this book.

No one wants to read your script. No one.

What they want to do is watch it.

**Screenplays are not meant to be <u>read</u>;
they're <u>meant to be seen.</u>**

We, as writers, never describe a scene, we *visualize* it. We write to the reader's mind, not their eyes. Just like a great novel does. The thing is though, we have fewer words and space to do it, and people want the story opened and closed in two hours or (preferably) less. We have to be very, very intentional with the words we choose, even down to how things lay out on a page.

What do I mean by that? Well, my next point is this: *what's not* on the page is a lot more important than *what is* on the page. The first thing, no joke, I mean <u>the first thing</u>, people look at when handed a script is "how much white is there on the page?" if the pages are heavily loaded with blocks after blocks of text, and long multiline parentheticals…they know right off the bat they're dealing with a first timer, and you've just wasted your toner.

Now, there's nothing wrong with being a first timer, nothing at all, just don't look like one. That's why you're reading this book.

And this "white space" is crucial in the horror space, even more than in other genres, why? There's a good chance you're going to have some (or a lot of) mythos/backstory to establish in your script. Maybe you need to tell a tale about how they never found the killer, or how the house on top of the hill was built on sacred Indian burial ground. These scenes need proper exposition, and the last thing you want to do is make large ugly blocks of text to get those points across. Hence, the *Rule of Three*.

Even this book has been written with this in mind. I spent many hours making sure this book works great on the page, not too much type, not too many rambling sentences, conversational but informative, just like me. I wanted the pages to look good and have a flow that could keep you engaged in the content. If you're the type of reader I am, I'm hopeful that if you've read this far, my work and style has kept you engaged and interested. But, if it hasn't, I'm sure I'll hear about it.

To help you understand how to be effective and ensure your first draft isn't complete rubbish, let me share with you a concept that's become second nature to me in writing, which can help you objectively whip your draft into the most presentable shape with plenty of healthy white on the page. It called...

THE WICKED PASS

After you've completed Act III, heave a breath of relief for completing A COMPLETE FIRST DRAFT. Congratulations! Now it's time to put it completely away for 24 – 48hrs. Just walk away for a break.

After those two days have passed, but before it goes out for initial feedback (which we'll get to next), it's time to take one last pass, which I call the "Wicked Pass." The *Wicked Pass* is essentially a thorough and complete review of your draft with a fresh set of objective lenses as if reading it for the first time. The purpose of this pass is to insure that your draft brings meaningful characters to life, creates visual images and actions that jump off of the page, and uses the most appropriate words that have been perfectly placed on the page. Sounds really complicated, but I promise you, it's not.

The more you do it, the better you get at it.

EXAMPLE: The Wicked Pass

<u>BEFORE</u>

EXT. HAUNTED HOUSE – DAY

The winter snow is white. The house on the hill is black and grey, with a slanted roof. Its windows are black with dust and age. A large moon rises up as night starts to darken the sky.

That's a decent action line, and nothing is technically wrong with it, but it's descriptive and not visual.

Let's put it through the *Wicked Pass*.

<u>AFTER</u>

EXT. HAUNTED HOUSE – DAY

The cold chill of winter fills the air. High on the hill, the house stands like a sentinel, watching and waiting. The moon climbs into the sky warning that night has come.

See how much cooler the second read is? Can you feel it in your bones?

It pops off the page, and onto the screen, right? This is

the power of the *Wicked Pass*. And it follows the *Rule of Three*. It tells the same story, just in a more "wicked way." The goal of this pass is to give your draft a fresh look, insure the words you've chosen come to life visually. Replace flat and boring descriptions with vibrant ones.

That's really it.

By doing that you have a far more visual and thrilling script. You have a page-turner. Remember, when the powers that be read your script, they all want one thing, a reason to pass.

Don't give them a reason to pass.

Exercises

Step 7: Complete Your First Draft

★ ★ ★

1. Motivation: As it pertains to writing meaningful characters, revisit your character cards for each of your primary characters. Make sure you have created an arc (emotional, spiritual, physical, psychological) and journey, and now write down what motivates them. Is it revenge? Accomplishment? Ego satisfaction? Money? A prize at the end? What is their kryptonite / what will they lose if they don't achieve their goal?

2. Sounds: List three sounds that scare you. Write them down one by one in the context that scares you the most. The sound itself sometimes may or may not be scary, but the context can sometimes send chills. EX: Car brakes screeching loudly, vs. Car breaks screeching loudly as you approach a wall of completely stopped, unexpected traffic on a winding road. Choose three sounds and define each.

3. Proofing: Start your writing every day re-reading the previous day's work. Read the entire scene out load; action, dialogue, all of it. Use the voice and cadence you imagine for each character as you read their lines out loud. How does it sound outside of your head? Are the words authentic to each character's voice? What can you improve? Use this exercise daily on your draft to remind you where you left off, where to pick up, and to ensure your writing tone and style are consistent.

4. Identify your "go to" words by reading your draft. We all have them. Read through your draft and when you come across a word more than twice, write it down, and make a tick mark for every time it appears in your script. (EX: Bloody, dark, eerie, deadly, creepy) Write down the 5-10 words that you use most frequently in the draft and tick mark how many times you find them in your draft.

5. Take your list of 5-10 "go to" and now over-used words, and find 3 – 5 synonyms you can use to replace these, hand-selected for the scene or context they're in. Replace the redundant word with a substitute. Choose the synonym that delivers greater impact than your initial word choice.

6. Remember, writing is in the rewriting, so repeat these exercises as you work and rework your draft, through *The Wicked Pass.*

7. COMPLETE YOUR FIRST DRAFT.

Step 8:

Schedule to Complete

★ ★ ★

Deadlines – Two small words that when combined will either *make* your career or *take* your career.

Yes, it's as simple as that.

The popular thought is that a deadline is a creativity killer; that any time a "clock" is put on the creative process, then that deadline will take away the script's creativity. You know, there is a bit of truth to that notion, but without a deadline, you'll never finish the script, so nothing is killed, because nothing is alive. So, who cares?

It's obvious when you have an assignment that meeting deadlines is imminent. And it is. Time is money and producers issue deadlines to see work delivered from the writer and to test their commitment and professionalism. Many writers feel there's always a week or two past the deadline given by the producer that's acceptable to turn in their work, but nowadays, that's really the exception and not the rule. And it's certainly not the rule if you want to be a writer full-time.

I have made the mistake of missing deadlines in my career. I remember once while working on an action movie the script was due Friday. That Friday, I was on my way to lunch when I got a call from the lawyer of the production company. They wanted their script. I said, "You will, it's 12. I'm going to eat and then after I finish the *Wicked Pass*, I'll send it along. "NOT GOOD ENOUGH!" was her reply. She screamed so loud that it cracked my phone! She then ripped me a new one for like twenty minutes. Even though I didn't technically miss the deadline, I was still caught in the production line of fire.

A few assignments later, my agent called and told me (in a very nice yet really stern way) "to manage people's expectations" which is to say, "stop b*llshitting them and tell them when the script is going to be done and deliver it on or before the promised date." And I've followed that advice ever since.

Now, I know what you're thinking… you're thinking I'm going to skip this part of the book since I'm writing a spec and no one's waiting for me to turn this in.

<u>Stop right there!</u>

You're 100% wrong if you think this chapter doesn't apply to you. If you don't use deadlines in your personal projects, you sure as hell won't be able to handle them in paid assignments, because you won't get any! I'm not trying to sound harsh, that's just reality today. There's no job in the world that lets you turn in your work whenever you feel like it. Not one that pays you.

There's a great cartoon that shows what writers go through as their deadline approaches...an impending 8-week deadline. The first six weeks are spent doing nothing. The seventh week is spent panicking. The eighth week they start writing. Although that's funny, and spot on but it's no way to write let alone live, and frankly it's unprofessional and won't garner you any paid work.

Deliver your work on time.

Exercise

Step 8: Schedule to Complete

★ ★ ★

Develop your "Writer's First Draft" calendar. Realistically this can be completed in 10 weeks. To achieve this timeline, the benchmarks for a professional writer's typical screenplay schedule is as follows:

Days 1 – 14: Complete Steps 1, 2, 3, 4, 5, 6 in preparation for Step 7

Days 15 – 48: Complete Step 7: Complete Your First Draft

Days 49 – 55: Let it (and yourself) rest.

Days 56 – 70: Completes Steps 8 – 10,

Day 71: Draft Day! Debut your First Draft!

Step 9:
Gather Notes and Feedback

★ ★ ★

Okay, who here likes going to the dentist? Hands up! No one right? No one wants their teeth pulled; no one wants a stranger's hand in their mouth. No one likes the sound of the drill (add that one to your scary sounds list)! It's unpleasant and gross. It's also a ton less painful than requesting and getting notes on your script. Unfortunately, like getting your teeth cleaned, and reviewing feedback on your script, they're both really, really important, and necessary.

To be honest, I like notes (while I still barely tolerate the dentist), but I don't like *getting* notes. Every time I've gotten them while in meetings, I've been told I look angry. I remember a producer at Fox stopped the meeting abruptly, looked at me and said: "Are you okay?" I must have looked like a loon for him to stop the meeting. I said, "Yes, I'm fine. I'm just processing."

You see what I realized was, the creative mind (at least

most of them that I know) can only *transmit* or *receive* one at a time. And it's a rare bird that can do both (receive, process, think, respond), and I ain't one of them. I need time to digest the notes and let my muse, Irv, chew on them for a bit. And once I agree there's a problem with a particular beat, I am now reopened to and welcoming to receiving feedback and processing ideas that might solve that plot point.

And there are all kinds of notes, there are *local (micro) notes,* and there are *global (macro) notes.* Local notes are simple, for instance, the reader might lose track of a character during a scene, so you might need to go back in and do some punching up of the action lines to clarify what happened. No big deal.

Now, *global notes* or *tonal notes* you listen to but avoid like the freakin' plague. These are notes that will sink your draft, and add weeks of work to your budding writing career. These are the notes that might sound like: "It just didn't make sense. I didn't like the hero. What's the point of the second act?"…stuff like this is big and should be avoided at all costs.

Now, remember a few chapters ago when I said get the first draft written no matter what? Here's the exception: when you know you have a plot hole so big that Jack Burton can drive the Pork Chop Express through it… that type of plot hole should be filled before anyone besides you sees the first draft.

If the killer of your slasher film, *The Chopper*, decides for no reason to attack the guy with the magic sword, just so you can get done with the script, you have some work to do before your first draft is complete enough to ask for feedback. I shouldn't have to tell you this, right? You best figure out why the Chopper was there to attack our hero by going back through the script (repeat Chapter 7 Exercises if you must) and peering in clues or scenes that will *earn* the big climax you want everyone to watch.

Now, if your first draft checks all the boxes through completing *The Wicked Pass*, and you find you're getting some notes you don't understand, ask a few questions. The hope is, the reader you've picked to do the read has some ideas on how to fix these problems, not just point out the flaws or gaps or edit your typos. And this is exactly where a lot of writers get offended by suggestions. To them I say, *get over your damn self*! This goes back to something I said a while back, that some people don't want to work (as in rewrite), and the more notes you receive, the more work you'll potentially take on to deliver the best possible draft for the world to see.

It's important to remember <u>writing is in the rewriting</u>.

This is the motto I live by and get paid to work by. And you'll be amazed at how much better the second draft is against the first. It's like magic, honestly. The first drafts of anything I've ever written all have good bones but really bad acne. With a little sulfur wash and a lot of soap and water, the results look sharper and clearer with each passing keystroke.

It just now occurred to me that someone reading this book, is reading this chapter and thinking, "What about the girl in *I Spin On Your Grave 2?*" "Are you telling me (spoiler alert) that the bad guys would ship a girl out of the country in a flight case?" And my answer is, "I loved that beat." I thought it worked well because it was so bold. And I say this without being able to take credit for the beat itself. That idea was baked into the movie when I came onboard. The producers wanted to start the picture in New York and end it in Europe. I thought that was a bold choice, but please don't try this at home.

I will take credit for the flight case; that was my idea.

Exercises

Step 9: Gather Notes and Feedback

★ ★ ★

1. Take your reader out for coffee, whatever they want, you pay. Once settled and sipping, you ask "So, what did you think?" Then, BRACE YOURSELF. Make sure you take your lumps (the bad) like a professional. Get ready to hear the bad first, that's typical, and expect a lot of it. (As mentioned before, be mindful of your facial expressions while digesting these notes, especially if you are sitting in a meeting at Fox.)

2. Capture their notes in writing, all the critical notes, not just the ones you like or want to remember.

3. Don't take offense to the notes that are given, even if your favorite character or scene falls flat. Simply ask questions to clearly understand what's not working from the reader, and why, and be sure to detailed notes. DO NOT feel it necessary to try to solve the problem or respond to their

comments on the spot.

4. Be sure to thank the reader for their time in reading your work and providing feedback on your script before you wrap up and leave the table.

5. Go home, look in the mirror, remind yourself (good, bad, ugly) you're not a failure and all is not lost because… "Writing is in the Rewriting."

Step 10:

Get your Draft ready for the world...

★ ★ ★

Your script is done, so now it's time to gather some more professional feedback. What's the best way to do that? I know, I know have someone read it. What's that you say? You know a big-time producer and think you can get it to him because your kid and his kid are on the same soccer team? That's cool! Could be gravy, but hold your horses. There are a few things you must do before you drop the script to Mr. or Ms. Big and start shopping for homes in the Hollywood Hills.

You need to get a few rounds of feedback; the first one is your inner circle – the friends and family plan.

The second, are pros to semi-pros.

Gather their notes, tighten the script up with their input, then, and only then slip the script to Mr. Big.

Why? You ask. Well, you get one chance to tell your story, and you want to make sure it's the right tale.

We do a two-tiered read/feedback for one reason. And that's to get the best possible script.

You see friends will read your stuff, and they'll probably like it because you're talented and all, but they may lack the understanding to tell you where you're weak. Or they just might lie not to hurt your feelings. I hope that the latter isn't the case, but it might be. Trust me; I've read some humdingers in my time, and I've done my own bit of smoothing over.

Let's say in your notes round you got a few large global notes: like, we hate the hero (the protagonist), or we love the villain (the antagonist). The whole mess sounds ass backward. What to do then? Is the script trashed because you're getting the opposite reactions of what you want? Not necessarily. I said before a few global notes will sink you, but they don't have to. Not if you keep baling.

Years ago, I was developing a movie about Eliot Ness hunting America's first Serial Killer called *Nemesis*. It's a true story and one that was very, very cool and noisy. We (the producer and I) met with Fox, they liked the idea but didn't dig how scary it was… they wanted more of an adventure tone.

Now, *tone* in all its forms is a global note and when I heard that, I thought… "f*ck this, I'm going to Arby's. No way am I rewriting this script to make it *adventurous!*"

Come to think of it; I think that was also why the executive stopped the meeting and asked if I was alright… hmmm.

I mention this because, this was to be one of those "off the books" rewrites, and the ones you do for actors and such… it's common to have the writer take a pass at writing something without paying them. That seems to happen way too often if you ask me. After all, have you ever asked a plumber to put in another toilet while fixing your leaky pipe? No, you don't, but that doesn't stop producers for asking for free work.

In any case, writing your first draft into the second draft is inevitable, because (say it with me now) – 'Writing is in the rewriting.'

On *Nemesis*, in particular, my back was up against the wall. We needed to get the project set up, and the work had to be done, so I dug in. I went to Final Draft and color-coded all the scenes I thought I could save, purple. And then I color-coded all the scenes I thought I could save parts of, yellow. Then lastly, I coded the scenes that would have to be trashed, black.

Once this was done, I realized I had more purple than black, and if I closed my door and just ordered and devoured only Chinese food and Pizza, I could turn this script around in two weeks. It ended up taking three weeks, but I got it done. I turned it in, and the executive at Fox that liked the project was fired two days later. WTF, man?!? That's show business.

Now, my hope is, your screenplay that you've just written with the help from this awesome handbook sets the world on ablaze. And you become the next big thing, I really do. But, if that doesn't happen immediately... don't sweat it. Most of my career has been spent writing spec scripts that don't sell when I first write them but do down the road. Times change, wants and needs shift and development people at the studio get fired or move on.

Honest, happens all the time. That's what's great about your script. You put it on the shelf it's always there, and if its your first script your next one will be that much better.

Each time you write you get better at it, remember the whole "writing is a muscle thing" I said awhile back? With each new script you get better at your craft and your profile is raised.

Also, even though I don't talk about agents, managers and the business world of writing I will tell you this. In order to get an agent, a good one, you have to have a few writing samples, not just one. A good number to have is five, all in the same "wheelhouse."

5 more scripts are 5 more chances to make it big.

A *wheelhouse* means all the scripts are in the same genre. Someone with four or five solid horror screenplays is a lot more likely to get signed with an agency than someone with a sci-fi spec, a horror movie, a musical, a comedy and a coming of age story is just going to confuse said agent and market place.

Titles

Titles, holy sh*t are they important!

* * *

Welcome to my personal fly in the ointment, my chief bugaboo, the thing that keeps me up all night with worry... *the title.*

The first thing I have is the idea for the script. I flesh it out in my mind for a day or two, then the first thing I worry about is the title. And it can't be a sh*t title or an "Untitled Thomas Fenton" That doesn't work for me. Titles, like drafts, change over time, BUT I have to start with a strong title.

The reason why it's my kryptonite is that, as time goes on, it's getting harder and harder to title something, especially now with the vast amounts of TV and film being made. But the good news is, with horror, there's a lot of different ways to approach the problem.

Titles can be a sentence...
Last House on the Left

The Hill Have Eyes
The Town That Feared Sunset
I Spit On Your Grave
The Amityville Horrors
Friday the 13th
House of the Devil

To a single word...
Halloween
Jaws
Saw
Scream

★ ★ ★

Now, what I'm saying is, don't stop working on your script until you have the right title; just keep your working title in the back of your mind while working. Make it a priority on your to-do list – a good title does a lot for a script. One thing I like to do is, when I have the title I think might be cool, I print out the title page:

It's a weird trick, but if I like the way it looks here, and I like the way it sounds, it's a winner. I would like to point out this title: JERICHO HILL – is from a Johnny Cash song, although I didn't know it at the time.

It's a good example of when titling your project; the best ideas crop up from all over the place. Eli Roth and Michael Bay's 451 Media made a short, based on this script, it's called SLAY PER VIEW, and it's on the website, thescreamwritershandbook.com

I'd also like to add one thing here, under no circumstances should you have the WGA# on your title page. It's a sure sign of a first timer. To be honest you shouldn't even register with the WGA – the protection only lasts for 5 years. A copyright last your lifetime + 70 years! If you do register with the Copyright Office, don't put that number on your script either.

Just have a way to contact you if needed.

Once you have the title of the project, make it yours. My hope is the title you choose will help shape the movie in a pleasing direction. What if *Rosemary's Baby* was titled, Woodhouse? How would that have changed things? Perhaps the focus of the film would have been more on the family and less on Rosemary and her baby.

One trick I use is the LISTING TRICK. Just write lists of names, places, and thing… you know… nouns and adjectives and see what looks cool together. Just write anything that comes into mind, anything.

Adjective:	Noun:
Dark	House
Cold	Messiah
Violent	Creek
Hidden	Car
Sinister	Land
Haunted	Chip
Gloomy	Hill
Poisonous	Road
Terrible	Monkey
Bloody	Ice
Frozen	Days

Okay from that listing trick I see there are a few possible titles. Sinister Land sounds kind of cool. What about Haunted Creek? That's okay, too. I like Cold Car – gives me an idea for a guy carjacked and locked in his car, the carjackers leave him, and he has to get out of the truck before he freezes to death. Kind of a Ryan Reynolds *Buried* vibe.

Personally, I like *Terrible Monkey*.

Tips and Tricks

★ ★ ★

Here are a few tips and tricks I've picked up through the years. They're things that make writing a little less difficult, and even some act as stop breaks for bad habits before they begin.

★ ★ ★

WHITEBOARD

If you have the space in your work area, a whiteboard can be your best friend. Even better than a human friend because it won't borrow money or hit on your sister. It's the shiny white guardian that stands silent and still, waiting for you to tattoo them with brilliance. I use a relatively small whiteboard, 3'x4' on my office wall. It's a fast deposit of ideas, titles and random thoughts. I used to use post-its a ton, but they usually came unglued, and my cat would steal them. That f*cking cat probably cost me an Oscar!

If you're working with a partner, it's great to

whiteboard together and either break or organize your ideas. Also, the reason, it gets you out of your chair, and when you're sitting here for many, many hours, any opportunity to get your fat ass up, even if it's standing at a whiteboard, it all helps.

NEVER USE THE "B WORD"

Don't ask what the "B" word is. I won't say it. I've never said it. And it's never happened to me, want to know why? Because I never say it, that's why. If you talk about your failings, you give them credence and substance. You have to look at such events like this; you're not "B'locked" you're working through some stuff. Is that lying to yourself, you betcha' it is, and so what? As long as you're not B'locked, who cares?

HANG WITH OTHER WRITERS

Now, this is to me as much as it is to you. I'm a solitary type animal, so writing works well for me. So I have to make an effort to hang with others in my profession.

Back in '04, I used to go to a coffee shop called Insomnia on Beverly Blvd. in Los Angeles. It was a writer's hang. Everyone in there was working on a film or a show. I made friends and relationships there that I value to this day. Every time I meet up with those guys and gals, I feel empowered. And I will say, a little competitive.

A little healthy competition helps fuel and keep the fires burning. Now, you might not live in Los Angeles where everyone and their brother are writing a film, but no matter where you live, I'm sure there are writing groups that gather and maybe read each other's work. This is a great companion to the solitary existence of writing. I know for a fact my friendships with other writers have made me an infinitely better writer.

Also, when it comes time for the second draft, these friends of yours will be very helpful in getting the draft in shape. Also, I always, always go to writers that are better writers than I am.

It's like playing tennis. Do you want to play against someone that's worse than you? No, you don't. You want someone that can kick your ass and hand it to you. That's the way you become a better tennis player, and that's the way you become a better writer.

★ ★ ★

GET A CAT

So you can pitch your stories to something that will listen to the rough ideas and help shape them without so much input they bigfoot the project. Why a cat? I'll tell you. Parrots give too many notes. Dogs tend to be too commercial. Alligators don't want to hear it. Cats are hard to impress much like your average Creative Executive and XYZ Production Company.

**Ask H.P. Lovecraft; he knows
what I'm talking about.**

Other Valuable Reads

★ ★ ★

Wait. What books to read? Isn't this the only book I need? Nope, it's not. It's a great one, but it's not the only one. In this book, we talk about writing genera horror films, and I assume you know the basics, and if you don't, then read these books below to get the basics.

One is Pen Densham's *Ride the Alligator*. I know Pen. He's a good and talented man. He taught me a TON about organizing my thoughts before I dive into a draft.

The only other book I'm going to mention is Stephen King's *On Writing* and that read changed my process 110%. King is a master in talking to his audience as if they were there, like the stories he shares are around the campfire, you can almost smell the charred weenies and smoke coming from the campfire. He again proves there's no alchemy to writing, nor any magic spells.

It's just work. I know I've said that before but I can't say it enough.

I would also suggest you read scripts of films that you like. Dan O'Bannon's STARBEAST a.k.a *Alien* is a fantastic example of a minimal use of words to paint a visual story. Also, (as mentioned before) a good read is *Lethal Weapon* by Shane Black. It's not horror, but its use of space, word, and phrasing makes it a very valuable read.

Trading in your daydreams is a tough racket. It's work. It's misery and joy. For anyone to pay you anything for writing words on paper is amazing, let alone enough to buy a pool.

It's a miracle, and man, I'm glad it exists.

Just for Fun

★ ★ ★

So, I'm not sure who wrote 55 things I learned not to do from horror movies , and it's written for laughs, but honestly, there's value in this list if you're going to write a horror film.

Take a look at 15, "*If your companions suddenly begin to exhibit uncharacteristic behavior such as hissing, fascination for blood*, glowing eyes, increasing hairiness, and so on, get away from them as fast as possible." Typical. Wouldn't it be cool if the whole "fascination with blood and hissing" was a *good* thing? Why not? Turn things on their heads, make it so. To survive the movie, the heroes have to become werewolves.

What about 47? "*If you're a male, get out of there as fast as possible! The only one who ever survives is a female?*" Use this to your advantage in faking your audience out. Make it seem like following the rules, but kill the girl at the end or make her he killer, that would be cool

★ ★ ★

55 things I learned not to do from horror movies

* * *

1. When it seems that you've killed the monster, never check to see if it's really dead.

2. If you find that your house, built upon or near a cemetery, was once a church used for black masses, had previous inhabitants who went mad or committed suicide or died in some horrible fashion or who performed necrophilia or satanic practices, move away immediately.

3. Never read a book of demon summoning aloud, even as a joke.

4. Do not search the basement, especially when the power has just gone out.

5. If your children speak to you in Latin or any other language which they do not know, or if they speak using a voice other than their own, shoot them at once. It will save you a lot of grief in the long run. Note: it's unlikely they'll die easy, so be prepared.

6. When you have the benefit of numbers, never pair off or do it alone.

7. If the gang plans a fun midnight party in the town's old abandoned mansion, don't tag along. Especially don't tag along if everyone's going as couples, except you're the odd guy/gal out. And if you're the gang's jokester, you may as well write up your last will and testament while you're driving with them to the place.

8. As a general rule, don't solve puzzles that open portals to Hell.

9. Never stand in, on, above, below, beside, or anywhere near a grave, tomb, crypt, mausoleum, or any other domicile of the dead.

10. If you're searching for something that caused a noise and finds out that it's just the cat, leave the room immediately if you value your life.

11. If appliances start operating by themselves, move out.

12. Do not take (or borrow) anything from the dead.

13. Don't fool with recombinant DNA technology unless you're sure you know what you are doing.

14. If you're running from the monster, expect to trip or fall down at least twice, more if you are female. Also note that, although you are running and the monster is merely shambling along, it's still moving fast enough to catch up with you.

15. If your companions suddenly begin to exhibit

uncharacteristic behavior such as hissing, fascination for blood, glowing eyes, increasing hairiness, and so on, get away from them as fast as possible.

16. Stay away from certain geographical locations, some of which are listed here: Amityville, Elm Street, Transylvania, Nilbog (God help you if you recognize this one), the Bermuda Triangle, or any small town in Maine or Massachusetts.

17. If your car runs out of gas at night, do not go to the nearby deserted-looking house to phone for help.

18. Beware of strangers bearing tools such as chainsaws, staple guns, hedge trimmers, electric carving knives, combines, lawnmowers, butane torches, soldering irons, band saws, weed-whackers or any device made from deceased companions.

19. Listen closely to the soundtrack; and pay attention to the audience, since they are usually far more intelligent than you can ever hope to be.

20. Never, never, NEVER try to communicate with something icky because "there's so much we can learn from them."

21. Don't make fun of or play with dead things.

22. If you find a town which looks deserted, it's probably for a reason. Take the hint and stay away.

23. If a meteor strikes nearby, move out of town.

24. When something bad is chasing you, bear in mind that when you try to start your car, no matter how

reliable the vehicle is normally, you'll have to crank the engine over many times before it will fire up.

25. If you walk into the local, abandoned-looking church to seek help or shelter, and you notice that the crucifix is mounted upside down, turn around and go back outside as quietly as possible.

26. When you happen to be one of the fortunate ones and actually make it through the film alive, never, NEVER sign on to do a sequel. If you do, expect to depart this world in the first five minutes.

27. Never have sex in the bunk beds of recently renovated summer camps.

28. Strange lights are seldom harbingers of joy.

29. People arriving to rescue you generally get ambushed by the monster, so don't rely on them as your only means of escape. In fact, expect to be surprised and delayed by encountering their flayed corpse at some point.

30. On no account should you do ANYTHING because someone dares you to.

31. If you realize that the people in your town/county are having their minds taken over by some strange force, alien or otherwise: DO NOT call the police as they are;

    1. either already taken over themselves and will turn you in or
    2. will not believe you and laugh at you. Either way, you must handle the problem yourself.

32. If a small band of children appears to be smarter than the adults that are around them, be cautious. If they stay together in a small, secretive group, and display nothing but hostility toward their elders, authority, and the church, leave town at once. If you wish to stay, be as kind to the children as possible, but expect to die anyway because you are inferior to them.

33. If you assist the villain of the film, do not expect gratitude in exchange for your services. In fact, do not expect anything other than death, which will come in the final minutes of the film and usually over the girl you have become attracted to, but the villain wants as their own.

34. If any animals, such as Birds, Piranha, Spiders, etc. begin to exhibit behavior that seems a bit more hostile toward mankind than normal, immediately call in the authorities, get out of that town, and do not try to talk to any scientist who specializes in that animal (ornithologists and the like) for they will not believe you.

35. Whatever you do, DO NOT keep pets such as cats, dogs, hamsters, or anything cuddly. If you must, do not let them out of your sight for as much as a second.

36. When you land on a distant planet and find some objects that look like eggs, leave them alone.

37. When one of your spaceship's crew finds a hideous

parasite attached to his body (as a result of disobeying the previous rule), don't let him back on the ship. The guy's dog meat anyway.

38. When a hideous alien menace is hunting you (as a result of disobeying the previous two rules) never wander off alone to hunt for the ship's cat.

39. Never, EVER go in/out there (There being the attic, closet, barn, basement, dark alley, dark anywhere else, the all-concealing shadows, the woods or the lake).

40. If someone who seems important tells you to do or NOT do something (like DON'T fall asleep, DON'T leave me, and DON'T look for the homicidal-chainsaw-wielding-psychopath by yourself) by all means, listen to them, unless doing so would break another of the guidelines.

41. If you manage to lose a few body parts along the way, don't despair. Take this opportunity to replace them with weapons, such as chainsaws, harpoons, etc.

42. If you are using a gun to combat the all-consuming evil, it is a good idea to quickly find a new means of defense, because no matter how much ammo you have, you'll run out just before you kill the monster (unless your name is Ash, in which case, you'll never have to reload).

43. If you are wounded by flesh-eating zombies, abandon all hope, because sooner or later, no matter how many antibiotics you take, yer gonna become

one of 'em.

44. If you're the last main character left, and a bunch of people is hunting the monster/monsters, DON'T stand out in the open because you will immediately be mistaken for a/the monster.

45. Don't open your closed door, especially if you hear scratching, heavy breathing, or any other strange noises from the other side.

46. DO NOT go into the dark room.

47. If you're a male, get out of there as fast as possible! The only one who ever survives is a female.

48. While in a horror film, never bathe, especially when in the house alone.

49. Regarding weaponry and general equipment for fighting the monster, never rely on any tool more complicated than a pointed stick. Generators will inexplicably run out of power, just as the nasty space-vegetable climbs onto your jury-rigged electrical grid. Just when you've got the ghoul lined up in your sights, your gun will invariably jam.

50. If you are a female, never show your breasts, easy women are expendable.

51. Never camp or build homes on Indian burial grounds.

52. Ask why the estate is being sold so cheap.

53. If the phone lines are dead, and you hear footsteps upstairs, when you're supposed to be alone,

don't follow the noises to see who your "guest" is. LEAVE IMMEDIATELY. Unless you want to die!!

54. Never pick up the phone and call for help, chances are your phone will be dead and the next thing you'll see is the monster swinging some sort of sharp object.

55. If you have defeated the monster, pay close attention to the camera, if it pans away for no apparent reason at all, get the heck out of there.

Parting Words
I'm here if you need me.

So, it's the end of this book. And my hope is, you've gotten your money's worth. And if you haven't, I want to know. If you hated the book or loved the book, please let me know. You can email me at Tom@thescreamwritershandbook.com.

One thing though, don't send me any unsolicited stories. If you're smart enough to buy this book, you're smart enough to have great ideas, and I don't need the legal headaches, I have enough of those already.

So, take care, and good writing.
Thomas Fenton

But if by chance you're looking for a little more aggressive and hands-on experience, I offer MASTER MINDS, an intensive course that will make your script that much better. Master Minds is offered to a small group of writers that I feel have the ambition and talent to take things to the next level.

Visit thescreamwritershandbook.com for more info.

SAW IV

by
Thomas Fenton

Writer's first draft

12 07 06

Inside a silent black void. Endless. Deep. Cold.

We hear a HEARTBEAT growing, thumping in slow patient rhythm. The sound gets louder.

The heartbeat carries through the following scenes growing in volume over time:

                                        FLASH CUT TO:

     - MONTAGE OF THE LAST MOMENTS OF SAW 3 -

INT. JIGSAW'S SICK ROOM - SAW 3 - EXISTING

Amanda squares off with a frightened Lynn. Jigsaw watches from his hospital bed.

                    LYNN
          Why are you doing this to me?

                    AMANDA
          It's simple. He stays alive...

                                        FLASH CUT TO:

INT. JIGSAW'S SICK ROOM - SAW 3 - EXISTING

JIGSAW coughing up blood during his seizure.

                                        FLASH CUT TO:

INT. JIGSAW'S SICK ROOM - SAW 3 - EXISTING

Amanda leans into Lynn threateningly.

                    AMANDA (V.O.)
          ...you stay alive.

                                        FLASH CUT TO:

INT. JIGSAW'S LAIR - SAW 3 - EXISTING

Amanda hanging the strange KEY (Master Key) around her neck.

                    JIGSAW (V.O.)
               In the end, she will be the closest I've
               ever come to a daughter of my own.

                                         FLASH CUT TO:

INT. JIGSAW'S SICK ROOM - SAW 3 - EXISTING

Amanda stands by Jigsaw's death bed.

                    JIGSAW
               I need you to do something for me.

INT. JIGSAW'S LAIR - SAW 3 - EXISTING

AMANDA reads from the mysterious ENVELOPE.

                    JIGSAW (V.O.)
               Start by looking in the envelope in my
               desk.

What she reads sends her into a rage.

                                         FLASH CUT TO:

INT. JIGSAW'S SICK ROOM - SAW 3 - EXISTING

JIGSAW eyes Amanda from his bed. Lynn stands close by.

                    JIGSAW
               Let her go.

                    AMANDA
               No!

Amanda holds the gun firm in her fist. Her eyes swimming
in torment.

                    AMANDA (CONT'D)
               No one learned anything from your tests!

                                         FLASH CUT TO:

INT. JIGSAW'S SICK ROOM - SAW 3 - EXISTING

JIGSAW pouring candle wax onto the TAPE from his bedside.

                                         FLASH CUT TO:

As Amanda lays on the ground dying. Jigsaw lays at death's doorway.

JIGSAW
You never tested anyone...

FLASH CUT TO:

INT. BATHROOM - SAW 3 - EXISTING

AMANDA suffocating Adam with the plastic bag.

JIGSAW (V.O.)
You simply killed them.

FLASH CUT TO:

INT. JIGSAW'S SICK ROOM - SAW 3 - EXISTING

Jigsaw's voice strains with emotions.

JIGSAW
I was testing you.

FLASH CUT TO:

INT. JIGSAW'S SICK ROOM - SAW 3 - EXISTING

Jeff swings the buzzing blade over Jigsaw's neck. Blood gushes out in waves. In Jigsaw's hand is a tape player.

VOICE
...I was your last test of forgiveness...

Jeff screams out. Jigsaw's eyes close. The TAPE PLAYER slips from his fingers and falls to the floor.

The thunderous heartbeat stops...

Lynn's trap fires - leaving a bloody smoldering mess.

The door to the sick room slams closed with a thick solid THUD.

SMASH CUT TO BLACK:

Silence... so quiet you can hear your own breath.

Then...

                    AMANDA (V.O.)
               What is the key to immortality?

                         JIGSAW (V.O.)
                    A life worth remembering.

An electronic death tone of the EKG flat lining sharpens
into a piercing wail.

                                             FLASH CUT TO:

A blast of rusty light...

Close in: metal working against metal. The strain of
mechanics set into motion. The mechanics answering the
orders of the electronic death tone.

                                             FLASH CUT TO:

MONTAGE:

Gears bloody with rust and oil, crank to life its sharp
teeth feeding into the gears.

                                             FLASH CUT TO:

Gears feeding into cogs. Cogs turning wheels.

                                             FLASH CUT TO:

A machine grinds to life.

                                             FLASH CUT TO:

Rapid fire images: Warm blood. A glass eye. A wooden
smile. The DOLL laughing. Sickly white skin.

                                             FLASH CUT TO:

INT. MASHER ROOM - NIGHT

The cogs and wheels crank back on large springs, coiling
up with power.

WIDER: THE COGS AND GEARS belong to a device. A CHAIR
that is winding up with some strange power - and dark
purpose.

Zzzzaappppp - An arc of electricity sizzles...

A man's voice screams out.

                    MAN
          Heeeelllppp!

                                        FLASH CUT TO:

A SET OF EYES snap open. Buzzed awake by the jolt of
electricity.

Another scream of pain.

                                        FLASH CUT TO:

A MAN'S FACE drenched with sweat. His eyes dart back and
forth in fear.

                    MAN (CONT'D)
          What is going on?!

                                        FLASH CUT TO:

INT. A COLD ROOM - CONTINUOUS

A tiny cell sized chamber. Wet walls. Dripping water.
Paint peeling like diseased skin. A single naked light
bulb ebbs to life, hanging on a crooked finger of wire.

Set in the middle of the chamber is the device, a CHAIR,
with the winding gears and tightening springs. The Chair
is tipping up, bringing itself erect.

The chair is called, THE MASHER.

Strapped tightly to the Masher is a naked man. He's the
owner of the frantic eyes. His name is DAVID GRACE (30s).
Leather straps hold his head tight. His legs are
immobile. However, his arms are free.

THE MASHER'S gears crank back on springs, the width of
his arm. These types of springs are used in semi truck
suspensions, able to take the force of many tons.

The loaded power in the flexed spring, shudder with
energy awaiting release.

                    GRACE
          What...? FUCK! What is this!

Instinctively, he tries to climb out of the chair. He
can't. However, his free forearms don't have enough reach
to do any good except to touch...

                                        FLASH CUT TO:

What looks like a "DESK" - an angled sheet of steel. The surface of the desk is pock marked with ten "finger holes." Along the desk's side are sharp and rusty saw blades.

                        GRACE (CONT'D)
        What the fuck is going on!!! What is all
        of this!

The Masher's gears stops winding, when Grace comes to the upright seated position.

                        GRACE (CONT'D)
        Help me! HELP!

                                                FLASH CUT TO:

In the dark - a TV springs to life. Grace's eyes dart over to it.

The screen is adrift with thick white digital snow...

                                                FLASH CUT TO:

GRACE mummers as he stares, eyes wide at the television.

                                                FLASH CUT TO:

The television's speakers hiss and crackle with static...

Moments build upon moments... we wait to see what will appear...

                                                FLASH CUT TO:

Cold tears well in Grace's eyes.

                        GRACE (CONT'D)
        This can't be real. It can't be real!

                                                FLASH CUT TO:

The static skips to black. A familiar DOLL'S FACE melts into view.

                             DOLL
        Rise and shine, David. I want to play a
        game.

Grace's face wrenches in fear. He knows what's in store.

                        GRACE
        NO!!!!!!

The Doll's malevolent gaze looks at Grace.

                         DOLL
               For years you have done everything in
               your power to help those who hurt others.
               Your law firm helps the wicked escape
               their just rewards. How many hours have
               you sat at your desk working to free
               those who are undeserving of it?

                         GRACE
               Please. No...

                         DOLL
               They say the pen is mightier than the
               sword. How many lies have you written
               with a pen grasped in your fingers?

                         GRACE
               No... NO!!! I didn't do anything wrong!

A growing frenzy is building in Grace's eyes, as his mind fights to gain its footing in this cold reality.

                         BILLY
               As you can see in front of you are ten
               small holes... the size of a finger. To
               live, all you need to do is place all
               your fingers in the holes at the same
               time. But be careful, the edge of the
               plate is sharp and rusty, it would be a
               shame if you cut yourself. If you do not
               complete the task, the chair that you are
               sitting in will fold flat... with you
               with it.
                         (beat)
               Live or die. Make your choice.

A geared CLOCK on the desk starts. The countdown has begun.

The restraints allow just enough movement for Grace to reach the finger holes.

He puts in his pinkie fingers first. He strains his index fingers to reach the other holes.

He then makes a gruesome discovery...

The holes are too far apart. There's no way he can complete the task - with his fingers attached to his hands.

THE CLOCK marches on the two minutes dissolving quickly,

FLASH CUT TO:

The rust worn SAW BLADES lining the sides of the desk.

FLASH CUT TO:

Grace comes to realize what he must do to survive this...

GRACE
No!!!!!!!!!

FLASH CUT TO:

THE CLOCK continues its steady march forward.

FLASH CUT TO:

Grace's right palm tests the rusty blades for edge. His palm slices clean and deep.

FLASH CUT TO:

The CLOCK winds away. He's loosing time.

FLASH CUT TO:

Grace braces his right hand with his left. His breath choking out of his throat. He places his hand on the saw blades.

With a deep scream. He draws his fingers over the blades.

FLASH CUT TO:

CLOSE IN: The skin of the fingers cut and tear. Warm fresh blood coating the raw sharp teeth. He screams. He runs his hand back and forth. More blood. More torment.

FLASH CUT TO:

The CLOCK has ninety seconds left on it.

FLASH CUT TO:

Grace's working his fingers over the blade. The cut grows deeper. Muscle tissue rips as the blades eat into his bone. He screams come louder, from a darker place.

                    GRACE (CONT'D)
          GOD HELP ME!

                                        FLASH CUT TO:

The cutting saw blades are coated with blood, pink
strings of muscle and chips of white bone.

                                        FLASH CUT TO:

Grace yells out as his PINKY FINGER is cut through the
bone. It hangs onto his hand from a ragged thread of
skin. He grabs it. Pulls. The finger is plucked free.

                                        FLASH CUT TO:

Grace jams his severed finger in the first hole, a
tattered spine of bone jutting from its bottom.

                                        FLASH CUT TO:

He continues working. A new wash of sweat, not from
fear, but from the exertion of the job breaks over his
forehead.

                                        FLASH CUT TO:

TWO MORE fingers find their holes.

                                        FLASH CUT TO:

Then a third - his right hand almost clean of fingers.
Only the thumb remains...

                                        FLASH CUT TO:

The thickness off his thumb makes it a stubborn digit to
free. Until.. His clenched LEFT FIST hammers down.

The thumb pops off. A blind catch, grabs it before it
escapes to the floor.

                                        FLASH CUT TO:

The CLOCK has one minute left on it.

                                        FLASH CUT TO:

The other hand works on the blades. It's hard going as
his bloody right stump of a hand is little help.

                                        FLASH CUT TO:

Grace tightens his hand into a fist. And begins working
on the thumb.

                                        FLASH CUT TO:

Back and forth over the blades. More blood. More bone.
More pain.

                                        FLASH CUT TO:

The floor of the cell is slick crimson. A gang of RATS
emerges from <u>under the back wall</u>, to feast on the warm
meal.

                                        FLASH CUT TO:

The thumb is cutting. The muscles ripping. The bone
drips with warm white marrow.

                                        FLASH CUT TO:

The THUMB is freed. Jammed in a finger hole.

Bzzzzzzz...

                                        FLASH CUT TO:

The CLOCK strikes ZERO.

                                        FLASH CUT TO:

Grace looks up. Horror anew. He lost track of the
time...

                         GRACE (CONT'D)
            Please. No...

Silence - like the eye of a hurricane.

The only sound in the cell is the blood dripping from his
hands.

The silence lasts just long enough to allow Grace the
hope that this is all a bad dream.

Creeeekkkk.... creeeekkkkkkkk...

Grace's hope fades.

                       GRACE (CONT'D)
            NO!!!!

Swwwaaaaaapppppppp....

                                        FLASH CUT TO:

The springs fire. The chair jumps closed. The Masher's power is awesome.

Grace's knees shatter his teeth as they punch into his mouth. His rib cage crushes flat like a beer can under a heavy boot.

Any orifice that can, spits blood in thick squirts. Grace's hands are forced up by the violent energy.

The explosion of the Masher's energy is so great, a small piece of the device <u>breaks off</u> and clangs to the floor.

In the blink of an eye the man is flattened.

                                        FLASH CUT TO:

The RATS are gathering at the base of the device. Feeding on the blood. Not noticing that the screaming has stopped, and not caring that it has.

                                        FLASH CUT TO:

FROM ABOVE - looking down at the mess that was once the corrupt lawyer, David Grace. We center on his extended HANDS, the straps that held his arms in place, broken.

                                        FLASH CUT TO:

The RIGHT HAND a rounded paw of blood.

                                        FLASH CUT TO:

The LEFT HAND has a single finger missing, with four still in place.

We CLOSE IN on the remaining four fingers.

                                        EFFECT TO:

Title:
                        SAW IV

                                            FADE IN:

www.ingramcontent.com/pod-product-compliance
Lightning Source LLC
Chambersburg PA
CBHW052059070526
44584CB00017B/2256